2020
NASHVILLE
Restaurants

The Food Enthusiast's
Long Weekend Guide

Andrew Delaplaine

Andrew Delaplaine is the Food Enthusiast.
When he's not playing tennis,
he dines anonymously
at the Publisher's (sometimes considerable) expense.

Senior Editor - **James Cubby**

TABLE OF CONTENTS

Introduction

Every city has its own nickname. (Some even have more than one.) New York is the Big Apple. New Orleans is the Big Easy. Chicago is the City of the Big Shoulders.

Nashville is Music City, pure and simple. When you hear the term Music City, you only think of one town, and that town is Nashville.

While Memphis is a larger city than Nashville, Nashville is the capital of Tennessee. I never actually thought about that till I first arrived here. My initial reaction on hearing that Nashville was the capital of Tennessee was to think how odd that sounded. I'd only thought of Nashville as the "Country Music Capital of the World," which of course it is. Not as the capital of anything else.

Having been raised in South Carolina, I well remember seeing Minnie Pearl on TV in broadcasts from the **Grand Ole Opry**, which has done weekly shows since 1925, making it the longest continuously broadcast radio show in history.

Nashville is not only the center of the country music business, but for Christian music as well.

They city has outgrown its label as a purely "country" town. What makes it particularly unique is that it combines the best elements of a small town (people say "Hello" on the streets, the clerks in the shops are as pleasant as can be) with the sophistication of a big town (the museums are superlative, the galleries cutting edge, the restaurants are world class—repeat the words **Catbird Seat** and **Rolf & Daughters** to me).

The restaurant scene has exploded, and now features some of the most original cooking that stands up to the best that New York has to offer. Just look at what they're doing at the **Catbird Seat.** I find it particularly interesting that Sean Brock, who so successfully opened Husk and McCrady's in Charleston, opted to return to Nashville (where he once worked for 3 years at the Hermitage) with a local version of **Husk**. If Brock's presence doesn't say something about the food scene in Nashville, nothing does.

The bar scene also has greatly expanded, offering much more variety. As for nightlife, there's never been anyplace with so much music going on. Start at the **Bluebird Café** (the location of scenes in ABC's "Nashville" TV show, though they use a set that recreates the site) and then dig deeper.

The formerly down-and-dirty **12 South District** has bounced back big-time with eateries offering sustainable cuisine, trendy shops, a cutting edge atmosphere, making it one of the hotter new areas of town. Meanwhile, in what's now called **SoBro** (meaning that it's directly south of the famous Broadway honky-tonk area), once home to almost nothing, you can experience a whole new neighborhood coming alive as it changes day by day, with famous chefs opening restaurants and craft cocktails being served at new hotspots.

One thing I guarantee: You'll never get Nashville out of your blood.

The A to Z Listings

Wildly Extravagant
Sensible Alternatives
Budget Options

3 CROW BAR

1024 Woodland St, Nashville, 615-262-3345
www.3crowbar.com
CUISINE: Sandwiches/Bar Grub
DRINKS: Full bar
SERVING: Lunch/Dinner/Late Night
PRICE RANGE: $
NEIGHBORHOOD: East End
Popular locals' hangout with happy hour specials and
trivia nights. Bar menu includes delicious sandwiches

like the Steak Sandwich served with loaded baked potato salad. Excellent draft beer selection.

12 SOUTH TAPROOM AND GRILL
2318 12th Ave S, Nashville, 615-463-7552
www.12southtaproom.com
CUISINE: American (New)
DRINKS: Beer & Wine
SERVING: Lunch, Dinner, Closed Sunday
PRICE RANGE: $$
NEIGHBORHOOD: Belmont/Hillsboro

This is a popular spot for locals serving great food and cocktails. Their beer list is extensive, and I'd guess they have the biggest selection representing Nashville's small-batch breweries. The grill's menu includes everything from burgers to tacos, sandwiches and burritos. Menu favorites include:

Grilled Salmon and the Garlic Stuffed Roasted Pork Loin. Vegetarian options available.

400 DEGREES HOT CHICKEN

3704 Clarksville Pike, Nashville, 615-244-4467
https://www.400degreeshotchicken.com/
CUISINE: Chicken/Southern
DRINKS: No Booze
SERVING: Lunch & Dinner Mon – Fri, Lunch on Sat; Closed Sun & Mon
PRICE RANGE: $$
NEIGHBORHOOD: Bordeaux Area
Very down-market joint with zero décor. You could as easily put a hardware store in the uninspiring bland space this wonderful spot occupies. What they lack in imaginative décor, they more than make up for with the food. It's all about their hot (spicy) chicken and comfort food. Order from the counter and waiters will serve. Expect hot-hot chicken that's moist and

flavorful, but if you're sensitive, it just might blow the top off your head. (I personally can't handle it, so I get it toned down.)

404 KITCHEN
507 12th Ave S, Nashville, 615-251-1404
www.the404nashville.com
CUISINE: American
DRINKS: Full Bar
SERVING: Dinner, Closed Sun & Mon
PRICE RANGE: $$$
NEIGHBORHOOD: Downtown; Gulch
Located next to the **Station Inn** in a former shipping container (that's right, a real shipping container), this very small eatery (about 40 seats) offers a menu of modern classic European cuisine. Menu favorites include: Glendale Farms Chicken leg confit and Peach and Pork Ragout. The impressive Chef Matt Bolus runs the place, which features indoor and outdoor dining.

ARNOLD'S COUNTRY KITCHEN

605 8th Ave S, Nashville, 615-256-4455
www.arnoldscountrykitchen.com
CUISINE: Southern
DRINKS: No Booze
SERVING: **Lunch only**, Closed Sat & Sun
PRICE RANGE: $
NEIGHBORHOOD: Downtown
This place is always busy so expect a line. The menu changes daily with favorites like Chicken and Dumplings, Meatloaf, and BBQ Chicken and Catfish. Here you'll find authentic Southern dishes served in a "meat plus three" style (that's meat plus three sides for all you non-Southerners). You will dine family-style.

BATTERS BOX

43 Hermitage Ave, Nashville, 615-242-0910
No Website
CUISINE: Bar Grub/Comfort Food
DRINKS: Full bar
SERVING: Lunch/Dinner
PRICE RANGE: $
NEIGHBORHOOD: Downtown
Sports bar that caters mostly to regulars. Bar menu features pizza and traditional American comfort food. Great burgers. Patio dining available if you wish to escape the smoke-filled bar.

BELLA NAPOLI

1200 Villa Place, Nashville, 615-891-1387
https://bellanapolipizzeria.com/
CUISINE: Italian/Pizza
DRINKS: Full Bar
SERVING: Lunch, Dinner
PRICE RANGE: $$
NEIGHBORHOOD: Edgehill
Unprepossessing joint offering wood-fired authentic
Neapolitan pizzas and a variety of pastas. (Go for the

pizza, as I find the pasta quite ordinary and uninspired. Not so the pizzas, which are excellent.) Outdoor courtyard that's very nice in good weather. Reservations suggested for weekends.

BISCUIT LOVE
316 11th Ave S., Nashville, 615-490-9584
www.biscuitlove.com
CUISINE: Southern/American Traditional
DRINKS: Beer & Wine Only
SERVING: Breakfast & Lunch
PRICE RANGE: $$
NEIGHBORHOOD: The Gulch/Downtown
This locals' favorite is an offshoot of a food truck that offers a menu of Southern fare – breakfast and lunch. There's always a line but the wait is well worth it. Menu treats include: Southern Benny (a Southern take on Eggs Benedict) and Donuts (specialty donuts made with lemon icing). Mimosas are made from freshly squeezed orange juice.

BLACK RABBIT
218 3rd Ave N, Nashville, 615-891-2380
www.blackrabbittn.com
CUISINE: Tapas/Small Plates
DRINKS: Full Bar
SERVING: Breakfast, Lunch, Dinner
PRICE RANGE: $$
NEIGHBORHOOD: Downtown
Chic eatery in an 1890s building with brick walls and wooden floors near Printers Alley (where Nashville's publishing industry got started 120 years ago) offering a menu of New American small plates and

tacos. The owners wanted to simulate an early 20th Century vibe, with handcrafted cocktails and music (live acts every night, usually jazz, sometimes played on a century-old piano), but it's really quite modern. The wood-roasted rabbit sliders are just perfectly delicious. All breads are homemade, the meats are cured in the basement below and a lot of ingredients get the scent of hickory on the grill. As impressive as the cuisine is, the cocktails are the star attraction here. Try the "Lost in Hell's Kitchen" - an aged rum Manhattan. Large list of impressive cocktails.

BROWN'S DINER
2102 Blair Blvd, Nashville, 615-269-5509
www.brownsdiner.com
WEBSITE DOWN AT PRESSTIME
CUISINE: Diner/Dive Bar
DRINKS: Beer & Wine Only
SERVING: Lunch/Dinner
PRICE RANGE: $
NEIGHBORHOOD: Hillsboro West End
A no-frills family run diner that offers "honest to goodness" diner fare. Of course the menu features hamburgers, hot dogs, hush puppies, and frito chili pies. Winner of "Best Cheeseburger" awards for many years and rightly so.

BUTCHER & BEE
902 Main St, 615-226-3322
www.butcherandbee.com
CUISINE: American (New) / Southern / Middle Eastern
DRINKS: Full Bar

SERVING: Lunch & Dinner
PRICE RANGE: $$
NEIGHBORHOOD: East Nashville/ Edgefield
Casual eatery offering everything from sandwiches to Middle Eastern fare. It started off with the interesting idea of making sandwiches with the same approach top-flight chefs handle the farm-to-table concept: use only the finest ingredients, but do it not with white tablecloths, or fancy European-style cuisine—do it with sandwiches. "A gourmet meal between two pieces of bread" about sums up their attitude. Well, it worked, and now they offer a varied menu with some interesting Middle Eastern twists far beyond the sandwiches (which are still a huge draw here, no question). They have 2 bars here, one with stools facing a regular liquor bar and the other facing the kitchen. Raw bare-beamed ceilings crisscrossed with exposed a/c ductwork gives the place an industrial feel. Favorites: Snapper Ceviche and Avocado Crispy Rice. The Bacon-wrapped dates and Lamb meatballs are worth trying. Impressive beer and wine list. Creative cocktails.

BUTCHERTOWN HALL
1416 4th Ave N, Nashville, 615-454-3634
www.butchertownhall.com
CUISINE: Pizza, Mediterranean
DRINKS: Beer & Wine Only
SERVING: Dinner; closed Mondays
PRICE RANGE: $$
NEIGHBORHOOD: Germantown
Rustic-chic New American eatery featuring a beer garden for wood-fired & smoked meats. Favorites:

Brisket tacos and Smoked turkey breast sandwich.
Page-long selection of beers.

CAFÉ ROZE
1115 Porter Rd, 615-645-9100
www.caferoze.com
CUISINE: American (New)
DRINKS: Full Bar
SERVING: Breakfast, Lunch, & Dinner
PRICE RANGE: $$
NEIGHBORHOOD: East Side
Trendy café with floor-to-ceiling windows looking out into the street. White marble-topped bar gives the place a clean, sleek look. On the other wall of the narrow room is a long banquette below a bare white wall broken up by some unusual modern light fixtures. Not a single piece of art on any surface. This rather severe sounding look is actually very sleek, very cool. Offers an all-day menu of creative American classics. Popular brunch spot. Favorites: Corn fritters; Chili eggplant; Steak frites; Harissa Chicken (with creamy polenta); Pinewood Farms Grass Fed Burger.

CAFFÉ NONNA
4427 Murphy Rd, 615-463-0133
www.caffenonna.com
CUISINE: Italian
DRINKS: Wine & Beer
SERVING: Dinner, Closed Sundays
PRICE RANGE: $$
NEIGHBORHOOD: Sylvan Park

Long-time no-frills locals' favorite for classic Italian fare. Where you go when you want basic Italian comfort food in a simple atmosphere. Dark enough at night so it can actually feel intimate, though there's nothing distinctive about the décor. Favorites: Fettuccine Alfredo and Lasagna Bolognese. The Tiramisu is a must-try, but my favorite was the Pumpkin ricotta cheesecake. Small basic wine list.

CAPITOL GRILLE
THE HERMITAGE HOTEL
231 Sixth Ave N, Nashville, 615-345-7116
www.thehermitagehotel.com
CUISINE: American
DRINKS: Full Bar
SERVING: Breakfast (from 6:30), Lunch & Dinner daily
PRICE RANGE: $$$$
NEIGHBORHOOD: Downtown

As I said above in the listing for the hotel where this dark-ceilinged dining room is housed, the Chef, Tyler Brown, who also owns the farm, grows the vegetables served here. The beef? Raised by Double H Farms just outside town, owned by the Heritage Hotel. Tyler changes his menus with the seasons to reflect what he can get fresh. Between the high arches are murals depicting Nashville scenes. House-cured country ham chowder; venison loin served with apples and parsnips; short rib pot roast; Brussels sprouts with bacon and brown sugar (I've never had Brussels sprouts served like this—just delicious); for dessert try the peanut butter chocolate chess pie served with banana ice cream and peanut brittle. Oh, and the charming **Oak Bar** located here, always an excellent choice for a drink.

CATBIRD SEAT
1711 Division St, Nashville, 615-810-8200
www.thecatbirdseatrestaurant.com
CUISINE: American
DRINKS: Full bar; $30 corkage fee (ouch!) if you bring your own wine

SERVING: Dinner Wednesday-Sunday; closed Monday & Tuesday; reservations from 5:30; last reservations at 9:15
PRICE RANGE: $$$$
They have a couple of booths against the wall, but most people want one of the 20 seats at the square-shaped counter surrounding the open kitchen, where the chef & his team make your multi-course meal (over $100 per person, but it includes wine and booze, so it's not as expensive as it sounds) while you watch. Whichever chef makes the course will deliver it to you personally so you can ask questions. There's no menu and you won't be able to find out what you're eating till you get there. But this is one of the hottest tickets in Nashville. It's next to the **Patterson House.** The food is exquisite, and if you can bear up to 3 hours to get through the experience, you will be handsomely rewarded. Expect items like: aged roasted duck; pork sandwich; duck breast with strawberries & almonds; hot & spicy chicken skins; crisp country ham; oyster with seaweed; snapper poached with chorizo; sea urchin with beets; charcoal grilled turbot. The desserts are standouts.
You have to reserve on their web site. Reservation dates open up 30 days in advance. If you cancel, you have to do so 7 days before your reservation or pay a $75 fee. Walk-ins are not accepted.

CHAUHAN ALE & MASALA HOUSE
123 12th Ave N, 615-242-8426
www.chauhannashville.com
CUISINE: Indian/Southern
DRINKS: Full Bar

SERVING: Lunch & Dinner, Brunch and Dinner on
weekends
PRICE RANGE: $$
NEIGHBORHOOD: The Gulch
Located in a refurbished garage, this dark room with
walls covered with red brick here and colorful tiles
over there has a lot of charm. High ceilings, exposed
beams on one side of a partition that divides the
room, with a white-painted ceiling on the other side, a
fireplace, quirky lighting fixtures overhead—all of
this adds to the fun, funky atmosphere. This eatery
serves creative Indian fare and comfort classics.
Favorites: Tandoori Chicken Poutine; Tandoori baked
brie; Hot chicken pakoras; Tamarind lamb chop; and
the award-winning Chauhan Burger. Impressive list
of wines and spirits. I'll wager you've never had any
of the desserts, so you'll want to order them all.

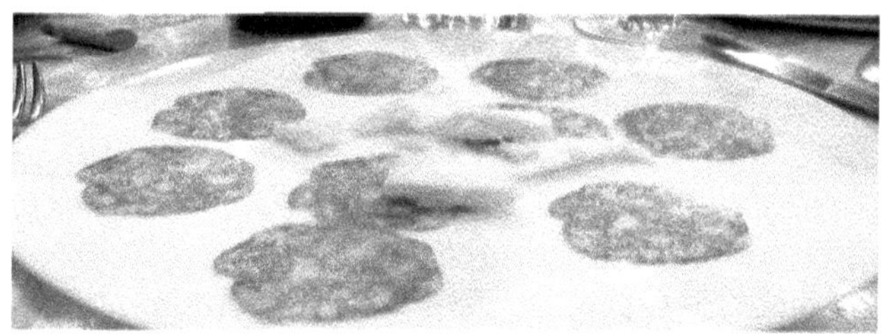

CITY HOUSE
1222 4th Ave N, Nashville, 615-736-5838
www.cityhousenashville.com
CUISINE: Italian
DRINKS; Full Bar
SERVING: Dinner
PRICE RANGE: $$$
NEIGHBORHOOD: Germantown

Chef Tandy Wilson has an Italian menu with a lot of Southern twists. He believes in the "snout to tail" approach when it comes to animals, and that's why he gets in whole pigs and uses every bit of them. You'll find his house-cured sausage in a pasta dish and then find ham from the pig's belly on one of his pizzas (the pizzas are unlike any you've ever had). Based on what I've said so far, you'll want to focus on the charcuterie items here in his big open room with brick walls that formerly was a sculptor's studio.

CRYING WOLF
823 Woodland St, Nashville, 615-953-6715
www.thecryingwolf.com
CUISINE: Burgers
DRINKS: Full Bar
SERVING: Dinner
PRICE RANGE: $$
NEIGHBORHOOD: Edgefield
A no-frills bar that serves burgers. There's a deck, a dart board and a juke box.

CZANN'S BREWING CO.
4909 Indiana Ave, Nashville, 615-748-1399
www.czanns.com
CUISINE: Pizza/Brewery
DRINKS: Beer Only
SERVING: Lunch & Dinner Sat & Sun; Dinner only Thu & Fri; Closed Mon - Wed
PRICE RANGE: $
NEIGHBORHOOD: Sobro, Downtown

This newly opened brewery offers a room for tasting its wares. No frills, no tours, and only 5 beers on tap. No dinner menu but they do serve pizza.

DINO'S
411 Gallatin Ave, Nashville, 615-226-3566
www.dinosnashville.com
CUISINE: Breakfast/Burgers
DRINKS: Full bar
SERVING: Dinner & Late Night
PRICE RANGE: $
NEIGHBORHOOD: Lockeland Springs
An old-school dive bar that serves cheap beer and burgers. Tip: Order your food at the register when you walk in and then find a seat. Beer and fries – that's the menu.

DOZEN BAKERY
516 Hagan St #103, 615-712-8150
www.dozen-nashville.com
CUISINE: Bakery/Sandwiches
DRINKS: No Booze
SERVING: 7 a.m. – 6 p.m.
PRICE RANGE: $$
NEIGHBORHOOD: Wedgewood-Houston
Simple counter-serve (pick up your order and go to a table) bakery featuring fresh baked breads (baguettes, sourdough, rye, challah and more) and sweets along with breakfast and sandwiches. Arrive early if you're pastry shopping. For b'fast, get a split baguette with Benton's bacon, scrambled eggs or just with homemade jam. Lunch could be a hot Cuban sandwich or salami or eggplant. It's all wonderfully

good. Try the fluffy Almond croissant and the oatmeal/cranberry cookie. Brunch served on weekends.

E3 CHOPHOUSE
1628 21st Ave S, Nashville, 615-301-1818
http://www.e3chophousenashville.com/
CUISINE: Steakhouse
DRINKS: Full Bar
SERVING: Dinner
PRICE RANGE: $$$$
NEIGHBORHOOD: Midtown
Upscale eatery with a friendly atmosphere in its dark and clubby room, with wood panel accents and flattering lighting scheme. I always get 2 starters here—the baked oysters (their garlic chili butter makes the difference) and the bacon wrapped dates.

They have a wide (and I mean large) selection of sides so be sure to inspect them carefully. Dessert, if you can manage it—the Apple Crisp Bread Pudding. Seasonal rooftop dining adds a nice element.

EARNEST BAR & HIDEAWAY
438 Houston St, Nashville, 615-915-1715
https://www.earnestbarandhideaway.com/
CUISINE: New American
DRINKS: Full Bar
SERVING: Lunch, Dinner, Brunch
PRICE RANGE: $$
NEIGHBORHOOD: Houston Station
Rustic tavern serving up American fare with a twist. It's a darkish room, rather somber, but has a lively bar scene. A few tables scattered around the room. Favorites: Wagyu steak; Burger made with Duck that's moist and more flavorful than their beef burgers, in my humble opinion. A couple of standout

items on this menu surprised me, like the lobster beignets, as well as the Hot Chicken & Mac. Excellent Poutine and Southwestern Soup. Good substantial cocktails.

EDDIE V'S PRIME SEAFOOD
590 Broadway, Nashville, 615-238-2359
https://www.eddiev.com/home
CUISINE: Seafood/Steakhouse
DRINKS: Full Bar
SERVING: Dinner
PRICE RANGE: $$$$
NEIGHBORHOOD: Downtown

Elegant national restaurant chain specializing in steaks and seafood. Oyster bar is great. Steaks are top-notch. I always get the seafood tower with oysters, lobster and shrimp (it's ridiculously expensive, I know), followed by the excellent ribeye cut. Live music. Happy hour daily.

EDLEY'S BAR-B-QUE
2706 12th Ave S, Nashville, 615-953-2951
www.edleysbbq.com
CUISINE: Barbeque
DRINKS: Full Bar
SERVING: Lunch, Dinner
PRICE RANGE: $$
NEIGHBORHOOD: Belmont/Hillsboro
Lovers of BBQ flock to this Nashville institution for the food and hospitality. Menu favorites include: Pork Tacos and the Catfish sandwich. The meats are smoked fresh daily and they also serve homemade baked beans, mac and cheese, and cornbread.

EPICE
2902 12th Ave S, Nashville, 615-720-6765
www.epicenashville.com
CUISINE: Lebanese
DRINKS: Full Bar
SERVING: Lunch, Dinner
PRICE RANGE: $$
NEIGHBORHOOD: 12 South
Lovely eatery featuring nice selection of Lebanese fare. Menu favorites include: Tabouli, hummus, and the Eggplant and lamb with vermicelli rice. Imported wines.

ETCH

303 Demonbreun St, Nashville, 615-522-0685
www.etchrestaurant.com
CUISINE: New American
DRINKS: Full Bar
SERVING: Lunch weekdays (11-2 only); dinner
nightly except Sunday, when it's closed
PRICE RANGE: $$$ to $$$$
NEIGHBORHOOD: Downtown
A classy, upscale restaurant serving food from what I
consider to be one of the top 2 or 3 menus in
Nashville. There's an open kitchen with seats at the
bar so you can interact with the staff (if you care to).
If you'd rather share an intimate meal with someone,
go to one of the tables. Scallops on a bed of greens;
octopus & shrimp bruschetta; rutabaga la plancha
(simply wonderful); a grilled lamb T-bone; tempura
okra; a sensational creation called the "Charcuterie

Salad" consisting of Tennessee prosciutto, house cured sausages, yellow beet mustard puree, greens, spiced vinaigrette, smoked lima beans, pickled onion, apple confit, fried oyster mushrooms—you've never had a salad like this before. The desserts are similarly creative: white chocolate lemon ganache.

THE FARM HOUSE

210 Almond St, Nashville, 615-522-0688
https://www.thefarmhousetn.com/
CUISINE: American (New)/Southern
DRINKS: Full Bar
SERVING: Dinner Wed-Sat, Brunch on Sun, Closed Mon & Tues
PRICE RANGE: $$$
NEIGHBORHOOD: Sobro, Downtown

Hidden gem with a fantastic menu. There's nothing to write about the interior here, but the reason for coming is the excellent menu. Favorites: Soft Beignets with blueberry sauce; Shrimp & Gouda Grits & Scallops (a nice twist on the traditional dish); sinfully rich deviled eggs (I never share these, and eat them all). Delicious cornbread.

FIDO
1812 21st Ave S, Nashville, 615-777-3436
www.bongojava.com/pages/fido
CUISINE: American; comfort
DRINKS: Beer & Wine
SERVING: Breakfast, Lunch, Dinner
PRICE RANGE: $$
NEIGHBORHOOD: Hillsboro/West End
This casual café offers a varied menu of organic, exotic and junk foods. Menu favorites include: the famous Local Burger (a mixture of beef & lamb) and the Liberal Salad. All desserts are made in-house. Breakfast is served all day.

FOLK
823 Meridian St, 615-610-2595
www.goodasfolk.com
CUISINE: American (New)
DRINKS: Full Bar
SERVING: Dinner
PRICE RANGE: $$
NEIGHBORHOOD: McFerrin Park
You walk by a stack of split wood on you way to the front door, and the scent tells you this wood is going to end up in the wood-burning oven where they make

the great pizzas here. Casual eatery offering a creative menu of American fare and pizza. But they have a lot more to offer than pizza: Chicken Milanese; Heritage pork with cranberry beans; Half chicken Milanese (this is very tasty); and Beef tartare. Get a side order of the marinated Cerignola olives. (One of my favorite types of olive.) Impressive bourbon list.

FROTHY MONKEY
2509 12th Ave S, Nashville, 615-600-4756
www.frothymonkey.com
Has other locations in Nashville
CUISINE: American; coffeeshop; sandwich shop
DRINKS: Beer & Wine only
SERVING: Breakfast (from 7 am), Lunch & Dinner (till 9 pm)
PRICE RANGE: $

NEIGHBORHOOD: Belmont / Hillsboro / 12 South
Very reasonably priced place for a meal any time. Not only is it cheap, but they're very serious about the sustainability of what their serve here. They have

gluten-free options, vegetarian & vegan dishes, a special kids' menu, craft-inspired beer & wine list. They support local vendors & suppliers. Look for the sign out front with the monkey holding a coffee mug. Biscuits and gravy with eggs; smoky asparagus & kale soup; French toast & waffles; great selection of salads and hot and cold sandwiches. For dinner, they have cider glazed pork with cinnamon sweet potatoes; blackened shrimp & grits; a sausage burger and blackened Gulf mahi. Also some great gift items from their store: crocheted monkeys and other items.

GIOVANNI'S RISTORANTE

909 20th Ave S, Nashville, 615-760-5932
www.giovanninashville.com
CUISINE: Italian
DRINKS: Full Bar
SERVING: Lunch & Dinner
PRICE RANGE: $$$$
NEIGHBORHOOD: Midtown
You can get really sublime Italian cuisine here. Giovanni is one of the stars of the burgeoning restaurant scene here in Nashville. An elegant room with white tablecloths and fine crystal with lovely arched windows looking outside. They have a traditional menu that touches all the bases, but what's special here is how expertly everything is prepared.

GREKO GREEK STREET FOOD

704 Main St, 615-203-0251
www.grekostreetfood.com
CUISINE: Greek/Mediterranean
DRINKS: Beer & Wine

SERVING: Lunch & Dinner
PRICE RANGE: $$
NEIGHBORHOOD: East Nashville
Casual no-frills eatery offering authentic
Greek/Mediterranean fare. Favorites: Athenian
chicken with peasant rice and Monastiraki-Style Beef.
Variety of Souvlaki skewers. Open kitchen and
communal tables. Greek wines.

**HAMPTON SOCIAL
NASHVILLE ROOFTOP**
201 1st Ave S, Nashville, 615-622-7772
https://www.thehamptonsocial.com/nashville
CUISINE: American (New)
DRINKS: Full Bar
SERVING: Lunch, Dinner, Brunch on Sunday
PRICE RANGE: $$
NEIGHBORHOOD: Sobro, Downtown

Located on the Hampton Rooftop, this eatery offers a lovely dining experience with skyline views of Nashville. The bright and airy décor is a perfect complement to the great views from up here. There's also an indoor-outdoor bar to go with the indoor & outdoor dining. Retractable roof. Bear in mind the menu is not that inspired; it's just OK, in fact. Come for the view. Favorites: Crab bruschetta and Braised Short Ribs. Delicious Key Lime pie that easily rivals the one at Joe's Stone Crab in Miami. Reservations a must.

HATTIE B'S
112 19th Ave S, Nashville, 615-678-4794
www.hattieb.com
CUISINE: American, Southern, Soul Food
DRINKS: Beer & Wine
SERVING: Lunch, Dinner
PRICE RANGE: $
NEIGHBORHOOD: Belmont/Vanderbilt

This place serves Nashville's "Hot Chicken" at its best. Menu favorites: Chick and Waffle special and Spicy chicken. Try the root beer float, a perfect combo with the chicken.

HENRIETTA RED
1200 4th Ave N, Nashville, 615-490-8042
www.henriettared.com
CUISINE: American (New)/Seafood
DRINKS: Full Bar
SERVING: Dinner nightly except Monday, when it's closed; Lunch Sat & Sun
PRICE RANGE: $$$
NEIGHBORHOOD: Germantown
Communal type eatery with wishbone chairs, a marble bar, a black sandwich board, offering a menu of small plates and elevated Gulf seafood from Chef Julia Sullivan who once worked with the famed Thomas Keller, but she definitely has her own ideas. Like the heavenly anchovy butter served with warm flatbread is worth the visit alone. . Or her roe mixed with sour cream and spring onions. Oysters (both coasts are represented) served raw or roasted with green curry, or stewed with cream and sunchoke. The snapper tartare is a marvel—ever-so-tender fish set off with crunchy lavender daikon, cucumber, serrano chile, toasted nori and crispy quinoa. Squid with fried polenta is accented with cured lemons and preserved tomatoes. Lamb sausage highlighted with olives smoked in a wood-burning hearth that's framed in tile. Other items I really like are the Cucumber Salad and Baked Ricotta.

HERMITAGE CAFÉ
71 Hermitage Ave, Nashville, 615-254-8871
www.hermitagecafetn.com
CUISINE: American, Diner
DRINKS: No Booze
SERVING: Breakfast, lunch, and late night. Closed
for dinner.
PRICE RANGE: $
NEIGHBORHOOD: Downtown
Certainly not to be confused with the grand
Hermitage Hotel, this old school diner serves your
typical diner cuisine including "breakfast anytime."
Menu favorites include: Veggie Omelet and Garden
Burger, but I wouldn't eat those—gimme the
sausages.

HONKY TONK CENTRAL
329 Broadway, Nashville, 615-742-9095
www.honkytonkcentral.com
CUISINE: American
DRINKS: Full Bar
SERVING: Lunch, Dinner & Late-night
PRICE RANGE: $$
NEIGHBORHOOD: Downtown
Very busy 3-story pub featuring live music. Menu is
typical bar grub like Tattor tots and deep-fried catfish.
Huge bar and pub menu. Large TV for sports fans.

HOUSE OF KABOB
407 W Thompson Ln, 615-333-3711
http://houseofkabobtn.com/
CUISINE: Persian/Iranian
DRINKS: Full Bar

SERVING: Lunch & Dinner
PRICE RANGE: $$
NEIGHBORHOOD: Woodbine
An eatery with a completely dull interior that happens
to have really good food (it better, right?) focusing on
kabobs with a selection of chicken, beef, lamb or fish.
All served with veggies & rice. Authentic Persian fare
like Gyros and Chicken Soltani. Popular take-out
eatery.

HUSK
37 Rutledge St, Nashville, 615-256-6565
www.husknashville.com
CUISINE: New Southern
DRINKS: Full Bar
SERVING: Lunch & Dinner daily; weekend Brunch;
indoor-outdoor
PRICE RANGE: $$$
NEIGHBORHOOD: SoBro; Downtown
Just as he did when he made waves internationally in
Charleston, Chef Sean Brock has brought his song

and dance act to Nashville. As the chef puts it, "In Charleston it's all about the
sea; in Nashville, it's all about the dirt." Led by Brock, the kitchen explores an ingredient-driven cuisine that begins in the rediscovery of heirloom products and redefines what it means to cook and eat in Nashville. The beautiful red brick building where Husk is located was built into the side of a hill in the 1880s by Dr. John Bunyan Stephens. Its storied history includes serving as Mayor Richard Houston Dudley's home, where he lived when elected in 1897. The area was settled by the Rutledge and Middleton families of Charleston who were descendants of two of the original South Carolina signers of the Declaration of Independence. The design of the Husk's interior spaces enhances the building's roots while demonstrating a sense of Southern style, modernity, energy, and cosmopolitan flair. The classic red brick architecture is enhanced with super high and wide single-pane windows that look outside through the graceful arches on the porch and fill the dining room with light. Menu changes daily. Try the 24-month old country ham with mustard and pickled okra; fried chicken skins served with hot sauce & honey (bring your Lipitor); pimento cheese with Carolina rice cakes; short ribs and beets; shrimp & octopus grits; fried chicken that comes with mac & cheese & cabbage; fried chicken hearts & gizzards; a good bet here if you can visit it more than once is to get the vegetable plate—whatever they have, let them bring it out.

JOSEPHINE
2316 12 Ave S, Nashville, 615-292-7766
www.josephineon12th.com
CUISINE: American
DRINKS: Full Bar
SERVING: Dinner nightly from 5; Friday from 3;
brunch on the weekends from 10
PRICE RANGE: $$$
NEIGHBORHOOD: Belmont / Hillsboro / 12 South
An elegant room with dark tufted banquettes against
the far wall under a few very large mirrors. Maybe
it's the lighting, but the crystal here just seems to
"pop." I love the big square bar. Grilled chicken
livers with pepper jelly; pickled shrimp; a great
selection of fresh veggies; noodles and dumplings;
pork jowl served with baby potatoes and pearl onions;
grilled catfish; beef cheeks with a horseradish risotto.
As tasty as everything else is, I invariably end up
getting the Josephine steak frites with a round dollop
of herb butter melting on top of the slices of meat.

Dessert? Try the sorghum molasses tart with brown butter. Also the peach shortcake.

KAYNE PRIME

1103 McGavock St, Nashville, 615-259-0050
www.mstreetnashville.com/kayne-prime
CUISINE: American
DRINKS: Full Bar
SERVING: Dinner nightly from 5
PRICE RANGE: $$$$
NEIGHBORHOOD: Downtown; Gulch
Handsome high-back banquettes against the wall. If you sit at the bar, you basically overlook a parking lot, but at night, when Downtown is ablaze with light, it's a different story entirely. 24-ounce bone-in rib eye is spectacular (you can take what you don't eat home); a black kale salad that's much better than it sounds; whole fish of the day grilled or baked; house-made bacon (with a layer of fat on it that makes it look like a side of pork (I won't even discuss the bacon topped with cotton candy that they serve here—it's scary); broiled trout; mac gratinee that's beyond delicious; duck tacos.

KIEN GIANG
5825 Charlotte Pike, Nashville, 615-353-1250
No Website
CUISINE: Vietnamese
DRINKS: Beer & Wine Only
SERVING: Lunch & Dinner
PRICE RANGE: $ - cash only
Superior Vietnamese specialties in this nothing fancy hole-in-the-wall. The staff may seem brain dead, but I think they're just overworked. Whatever. Whoever is in the kitchen is not brain dead. Get the BBQ pork bahn mi, or the very popular Pho.

LOCKELAND TABLE
1520 Woodland St, Nashville, 615-228-4864
www.lockelandtable.com
CUISINE: American
DRINKS: Full Bar
SERVING: Dinner from 5 (bar opens at 4) except Sunday, when it's closed
PRICE RANGE: $$$
NEIGHBORHOOD: East Nashville
Another one of those unassuming squat brick buildings you see
so often here in Nashville. Inside, however, there's a jumbled design that makes you think they weren't sure what to settle on.

Lights hang from the ceiling amid the industrial look created by the a/c venting. Metal barstools lined up against the curved bar overlooking the kitchen. Somehow it all works beautifully. Smoked Cox Farms bone marrow; pork & shrimp dumplings; chicken liver paté in a jar; hot crispy pig ears; a modest selection of excellent pizzas; rack of lamb; Niman ranch bone-in pork loin; the freshwater trout is particularly good. (Make sure you get a side of the crab & corn fritters.)

LOU NASHVILLE

1304 McGavock Pike, Nashville, 615-499-4495
https://lounashville.com/
CUISINE: American (New)
DRINKS: Full Bar
SERVING: Dinner, Brunch on Sat & Sun, Closed Mon & Tues
PRICE RANGE: $$
NEIGHBORHOOD: Inglewood
Located in a small, renovated white house serving a creative menu of American fare, you'll feel like you're going to Grandma's house for Sunday dinner when you walk up to the place. Very quaint, with a disused fireplace in the center of the main dining room. Out back they have seating on a porch that overlooks a backyard with an expansive green lawn. Favorites: Chorizo & Egg Sandwich; Skirt steak;

excellent Trout; Grilled Crab Cakes. Most dishes
meant to be shared tapas style.

THE LOVELESS CAFÉ
8400 Hwy 100, Nashville, 615-646-9700
www.lovelesscafe.com
CUISINE: American; Southern
DRINKS: Full Bar
SERVING: Breakfast, Lunch & Dinner
PRICE RANGE: $$
This is one of those places that's seared in the mind
of everybody who grew up in Nashville. This is a
"must" stop, even if it is a bit out of town. And yes,
the waitresses will call

you, "Honey.") Try to go early or after peak hours
because there's usually a waiting line, especially on
weekends. And no, it's not just tourists. These are
locals. A basket of biscuits comes with every order.

It's as Southern as you can get. Everything's made from scratch. You can watch them pull their famous biscuits out of the oven because there's a window into the kitchen. Ham & eggs with red-eye gravy. Ever had a breakfast with pit-cooked BBQ pork and eggs? No? You can here. Steak biscuits (these are very popular) using grilled beef tenderloin; Southern sampler (country ham, bacon, sausage and eggs). If you come for dinner, you'll be just as pleased, however: fried pork chops; grilled catfish; country fried steak; fried chicken livers or gizzards (I used to love these gizzards as a child); homemade meatloaf. All the sides are just perfect, from the fried okra to the mac & cheese. They have an extensive shop and they've been shipping their goods out for decades (now on the Internet). Get gift packs with country ham & bacon; pantry goods; apparel and accessories; gifts; biscuits; preserves; items for the kitchen. Also be sure to check out the **Motel Shops** located in what used to be 14 rooms of the original motel that was behind the café. Stop by to grab some of their jams and preserves to take home.

LYRA
935 W Eastland Ave, 615-928-8040
https://lyranashville.com
CUISINE: Middle Eastern
DRINKS: Full Bar
SERVING: Dinner, Closed Sundays
PRICE RANGE: $$
NEIGHBORHOOD: Greenwood
Casual eatery offering Middle Eastern fare with a modern twist. Favorites: Baba Ghanoush (Stuffed

eggplant) and Spiced hanger steak. Vegetarian options. Creative desserts like the Pistachio Ice Cream Sandwich made with a sesame tahini cookie. Nightly Happy hour with nice selection of bites and specialty cocktails.

MARCHÉ ARTISAN FOODS
1000 Main St, Nashville, 615-262-1111
www.marcheartisanfoods.com
CUISINE: Specialty Food
DRINKS: Beer & Wine
SERVING: Breakfast, Lunch & Dinner
PRICE RANGE: $$
NEIGHBORHOOD: East Nashville
Located in historic section of East Nashville, this European-style café and marketplace offers a revolving menu. Menu favorites include: Shrimp Grits and Pan Seared Pork Tenderloin and Cornbread

Panzanella. Breakfast served anytime. Great choice for weekend brunch.

MARGOT CAFÉ & BAR
1017 Woodland St, Nashville, 615-227-4668
www.margotcafe.com
CUISINE: French, Italian
DRINKS: Full Bar
SERVING: Dinner
PRICE RANGE: $$$
NEIGHBORHOOD: Five Points; East Nashville
This is a special little intimate place, and many people in-the-know think this is perhaps "the" best restaurant owned by a chef in the whole of Nashville. (That's saying something.) Red brick walls with lots of mirrors hanging on them; wood tables for lunch; white tablecloths for dinner. Chef Margot earned her strips in the East Village before returning to Nashville

to work at **F. Scott's** in Green hills. When she opened
this place, she focused on the cuisines she loves most:
southern France and parts of Italy, with an emphasis
on the hearty, healthy peasant cuisines of these
regions. The menu is seasonal and changes every day.
Homemade potato chips; Minestra with broccoli
pesto; pizza with veal, fava beans and ricotta; pan-
roasted redfish; grilled pork chop with squash
casserole. (To be honest, this is my first stop for
dinner when I get to town.)

MARSH HOUSE
THOMPSON NASHVILLE
401 11th Ave S, Nashville, 615-262-6001
https://www.marshhouserestaurant.com/
CUISINE: Seafood/American/Cajun & Creole
DRINKS: Full Bar
SERVING: Dinner, Brunch
PRICE RANGE: $$$
NEIGHBORHOOD: The Gulch/Downtown

Located in the Thompson Nashville hotel, this chic and sleek modern eatery offers elevated, seafood-centric Southern fare. Favorites: Oysters on the half shell; Salmon tartare; Deviled crab; Gumbo (shrimp, crab, andouille, okra); Soft Shell Crab is great here as well. Outdoor patio is an option in good weather.

MAS TACOS POR FAVOR
732 McFerrin Ave, Nashville, 615-543-6271
No Website
CUISINE: Mexican
DRINKS: No Booze
SERVING: Lunch, Dinner, Closed Sunday
PRICE RANGE: $
NEIGHBORHOOD: East Nashville
This popular "mobile eatery" (I love that term for a food truck) offers a creative menu of tacos and soups. Menu favorites include: Pulled Pork taco and Cast-

iron chicken taco. Great place for a fast weekend brunch.

MILK AND HONEY
214 11th Ave S, Nashville, 615-712-7601
https://www.milkandhoneynashville.com/
CUISINE: American (New)/Brunch
DRINKS: Full Bar
SERVING: Breakfast, Lunch
PRICE RANGE: $$
NEIGHBORHOOD: The Gulch, Downtown
Very popular, trendy coffee shop (expect a wait because it's always bustling). Impressive selection of coffees, pastries, and breakfast items. You can even order a Nutella Oat Milk Bailey's Latte. Deli-style sandwiches; large pizza selection; exceptional omelets; they have what they call "brunch sandwiches," which I love because you get about a

dozen types of breakfast sandwiches you don't see offered elsewhere

MOCKINGBIRD
121 12th Ave N, Nashville, 615-741-9900
http://www.mockingbirdnashville.com/
CUISINE: American (New) / Tapas (Small plates) / Diner
DRINKS: Full Bar
SERVING: Lunch & Brunch Fri – Sun, Dinner Wed – Sun, Closed Mon & Tues
PRICE RANGE: $$
NEIGHBORHOOD: Downtown
Upscale diner serving American comfort food with some creative twists. There's a nice long bar area when you come into the front room, with some tables and booths in the back room. (The bar is more fun.) Favorites: Barbacoa (Short Rib pancit Canton noodles & porcini broth); Chopped pork belly with fried egg;

Tatchos with lamb chili (delicious) cheddar spiced with beer and tater tots; also a Corn Bog that's a Bratwurst made with pork ginger. I had it and it was great. Took me back to my county fair days. Amazing pastries and breakfast dishes. Creative cocktails like the Punchin Bag.

MONELL'S
1235 6th Ave N, Nashville, 615-248-4747
www.MonellsTn.com
CUISINE: Southern; soul food
DRINKS: No Booze
SERVING: Breakfast (from 10), Lunch & Dinner
PRICE RANGE: $$
NEIGHBORHOOD: Germantown
I think the must use a shovel in the kitchen when they plate the food, there's so much of it. Excellent Southern food served family style. There's only a basic menu, with specials every day; Monday, chicken & dumplings & meatloaf; Tuesday, spinach lasagna and pot roast; Wednesday, pork chops, baked

chicken and fried chicken (they fry it in a skillet); and so on and so forth. Full country breakfast available. Excellent sides like fried apples, cheese grits, corn pudding. Whatever day it is, it will be good, I guarantee it.

NADA
202 21st Ave S, Nashville, 615-925-3362
https://www.eatdrinknada.com/location/nashville/
CUISINE: Mexican & other Latin / Breakfast
DRINKS: Full Bar
SERVING: Lunch & Breakfast Thurs- Sun, Dinner
Tues – Sun, Closed Mondays
PRICE RANGE: $$
NEIGHBORHOOD: Midtown, Music Row

Popular Mexican eatery with a clever menu. There's a pretty outdoor seating area with twinkly lights strung above you that make the place feel cozy at night. Those same twinkle lights are strung below the bar inside, so it's kind of a theme. Bustling place with a décor that's pleasing to the eye. Favorites: Fajita style veggie tacos; the Peruvian chicken comes either half or whole, and is roasted in beer; I had a couple of bites of my companion's Argentine-style cote de boeuf, which is an 18-oz prime ribeye crusted in ancho peppers which adds an incredible smoked flavor to the meat. Margaritas are top notch. (I had 4 last trip—thank God for Uber!) Reservations recommended.

OTAKU RAMEN
1104 Division St, Nashville, 615-942-8281
www.otakuramen.com
CUISINE: Ramen
DRINKS: Full bar
SERVING: Lunch/Dinner; Closed Mon
PRICE RANGE: $$
NEIGHBORHOOD: The Gulch/Downtown
Trendy eatery offering a menu of traditional ramen and Japanese fare. Nice selection of ramen – even vegetarian selections. Try the hot chicken bun appetizer – delicious.

THE PANCAKE PANTRY
1796 21st Ave S, Nashville, 615-383-9333
www.thepancakepantry.com
CUISINE: Bakeries, Breakfast

DRINKS: No Booze
SERVING: Breakfast & Lunch (6 a.m. to 3 p.m.)
PRICE RANGE: $$
NEIGHBORHOOD: Hillsboro, West End
You'll go crazy for the pancakes here—Swiss
chocolate chip pancakes; especially the sweet potato
pancakes served with a cinnamon syrup. There are
over 20 varieties, like Santa Fe

(cornmeal pancakes with bits of bacon, cheddar and
green chilis), the Caribbean (buttermilk cakes with
pecans, coconut, powdered sugar, slices of banana).
It's hard to get a seat at one of the Formica tables
here. The lines are very long, so plan on going early
or late at off peak hours. There's plenty more on the
menu if you're not eating carbs: sandwiches; burgers;
ham and egg plates, lots more.

PENINSULA
1035 W Eastland Ave, 615-679-0377

<u>www.peninsulanashville.com</u>
CUISINE: Portuguese/Spanish
DRINKS: Full Bar
SERVING: Dinner, Closed Sun & Mon.
PRICE RANGE: $$
NEIGHBORHOOD: East Nashville
Modern eatery offering the cuisines of Iberia. They had to add a few beams to the ceiling here in an effort to create a little atmosphere. High wide windows looking out to the residential neighborhood across the street are nice, bringing in lots of light. The place is simple, and just fine. The focus here is the quality of the Spanish and Portuguese dishes they offer, and they couldn't be better. Not what you expect here in Nashville. Favorites: Chick gizzards passion fruit, turmeric; Morcilla Crepe with sweetbreads and onion (very nice); Braised rabbit (this is a dish they are justifiably very proud of) with garlic broth & pimenton. Main courses: Pork Cheeks with Squid Ink. Interesting desserts. Impressive wine list.

PHARMACY BURGER PARLOR AND BEER GARDEN

731 McFerrin, Nashville, 615-712-9517
www.thepharmacynashville.com
CUISINE: American; Burgers; pub fare
DRINKS: Beer & Wine
SERVING: Lunch & Dinner daily
PRICE RANGE: $$
NEIGHBORHOOD: East Nashville
Just a square white building from the outside, but inside there's a good vibe where locals meet to eat fantastic burgers and drink beer. Has an impressive selection of German wurst and German beer. There's a Stroganoff Burger (mushroom stroganoff béchamel, sour cream, caramelized onion, Swiss cheese); among many others, as well as lots of German wursts: Jagerwurst, Bratwurst, Currywurst, Bauerwurst, Kielbasa, Bockwurst. Sides are handmade and uniformly excellent. Also there's an old-school sofa fountain serving up phosphates, milkshakes and ice

cream sodas. In good weather, sit in the beer garden out back under the string of lights criss-crossing above you in the leafy canopy. (The ice cream here is particularly good.)

PRINCE'S HOT CHICKEN SHACK
5814 Nolensville Pike, Nashville, 615-810-9388
https://princeshotchicken.com
CUISINE: Southern
DRINKS: No Booze
SERVING: Lunch, Dinner; closed Sunday
PRICE RANGE: $

Known as the pioneer of Hot Chicken, this place
serves a variety of Hot Chicken in pieces, strips or
whole. It's quite popular so expect a wait. The story
goes that back in the 1930s, Thornton Prince came
home very late after cheating on his girlfriend. To get
back at him, she gave him fried chicken loaded down
with cayenne pepper. Her trick backfired, because he
loved it. He even opened the country's first "hot
chicken" place in the mid-1930s. If you can handle
the heat, you'll find the chicken they fry is moist and
juicy inside. They will warn you not to touch your
eyes after eating this chicken.

PUCKETT'S GROCERY & RESTAURANT
500 Church St Nashville, 615-770-2772
www.puckettsgrocery.com
CUISINE: American
DRINKS: Full Bar
SERVING: Breakfast, Lunch, Dinner daily
PRICE RANGE: $$
NEIGHBORHOOD: Downtown
Great location in a corner building in Downtown. Not
only is it a good restaurant, but there's a store and live
music as well on the little stage on one side of the
dining room. Ultra-casual atmosphere. Your drinks
come in mason jars. Pulled pork sliders; fried pickles
& jalapenos; fried green tomatoes & chipotle dip;
cherry-smoked hot wings; Southern fried catfish;
Piggy Mac (smoked pulled pork in an iron skillet
topped with smoked gouda mac & cheese); smoked
baby back ribs. (Get the Maple Pecan Pie if you can
manage it after stuffing yourself with all this comfort
food.) If you're here for breakfast, try the Bubba's

Eggs Benedict (split biscuits topped with bacon or sausage covered with 2 fried eggs and smothered in pepper gravy).

ROLF AND DAUGHTERS
700 Taylor St, Nashville, 615-866-9897
www.rolfanddaughters.com
CUISINE: American, Mediterranean
DRINKS: Full Bar
SERVING: Dinner
PRICE RANGE: $$$
NEIGHBORHOOD: Germantown
This restaurant, run by Chef Philip Krajeck, offers a beautiful dining experience in a refurbished Werthan packaging factory that's a century old. It has brick walls, old slats of reclaimed wood on the high ceiling above and these tall wide windows with no drapes or

anything that gives it a workhouse look. At the long dorm style common table stretching down the center, you almost expect to see Oliver Twist eating his gruel. A great atmosphere. The Belgian-raised Chef Krajeck is famous around these parts not for his gruel, but for his fresh pasta. Among the more unique eateries in town, Rolf combines Southern food with a Northern Italian - Mediterranean twist. Menu favorites include: Crispy-Skinned Chicken; Pork Tenderloin; chicken-liver pate served with a green tomato jam; meatballs and dandelion greens.

ROSIE FOOD & WINE
203 Anderson Lane N, Hendersonville, 615-757-3305
https://www.rosiefoodandwine.com/
CUISINE: Italian/Seafood/Wine Bar
DRINKS: Full Bar
SERVING: Dinner; Closed Mon & Sun
PRICE RANGE: $$
NEIGHBORHOOD: Hendersonville
A short drive out to Hendersonville will bring you to this popular neighborhood eatery with a mixed-bag menu. Favorites: Pork Cheek Tortellini. Will melt in your mouth—very rich but also very satisfying; Short Ribs Braised in red wine; Homemade blueberry lasagna. The pork croquetas make a good starter. Nice wines and desserts.

SKULL'S RAINBOW ROOM
222 Printers Alley, Nashville, 615-810-9631
www.skullsrainbowroom.com
CUISINE: Modern American
DRINKS: Full bar

SERVING: Lunch/Dinner
PRICE RANGE: $$
NEIGHBORHOOD: Downtown
Located in historic Printers Alley, this eatery offers a menu of American fare, crafted cocktails and live burlesque shows (twice nightly). Menu favorites: Grilled salmon and Lobster bisque. Reservations recommended.

SOUTHERN STEAK & OYSTER

150 3rd Ave S, Nashville, 615-724-1762
www.thesouthernnashville.com
CUISINE: American; New Southern
DRINKS: Full Bar
SERVING: Breakfast weekdays from 7:30; Lunch daily; Dinner nightly (but bar opens for happy hour at 3); brunch on weekends from 10 am
PRICE RANGE: $$$
NEIGHBORHOOD: Downtown; SoBro

Has a very New York feel with its subway style bathroom white-tiled floor, expansive back bar and thin-strips of wood in the ceiling. This is a very good place for breakfast: Southern omelet (braised pork, onions, collards, black-eyes peas, cheddar, served with grits or potatoes); smoked brisket with jalapeno cheddar grits and 2 fried eggs; or the fried egg sandwich. Later on, I like the daily selection of oysters. They usually have two or 3 types. Also the Dominican braised pork; bahn mi tacos; double-cut smoked pork chop; baby back ribs; dry aged strip steak.

THE STILLERY
113 2nd Ave N, Nashville, 615-942-8080
1921 Broadway, Nashville, 615-760-5158
http://www.stillerynashville.com/
CUISINE: American (New); Sports Bar / Live Music
DRINKS: Full Bar

SERVING: Lunch & Dinner
PRICE RANGE: $$
NEIGHBORHOOD: Downtown / Midtown
Two locations. Small eatery with live music behind the bar and in the other place also on a small stage on the other side of the room. The place is bathed in a deep blue light when the music gets started. Everything here from freshly made pizzas to burgers, Fried pickles, and Catfish & Chips. Loved the Deviled Eggs. Reservations recommended/bar is reservations only.

STK STEAKHOUSE

700 12th Ave S, Nashville, 615-619-3500
Corner of Division St; 12th Avenue South
https://stksteakhoßuse.com/venues/nashville/
CUISINE: Steakhouse/American (Traditional)
DRINKS: Full Bar
SERVING: Dinner, Brunch/Lunch Sat & Sun
PRICE RANGE: $$$$

NEIGHBORHOOD: The Gulch, Downtown
Popular nationwide steakhouse with pretty much the
standard "steakhouse" menu of prime meats &
outrageously expensive seafood specialties. Here in
Nashville, the place has a vigorous weekday happy
hour filling the place to the max. Lots of energy, lots
of fun. Easy to meet locals here. Sleek modern décor
is one of the nicest in town. Favorites: Filet lollipop
and Parmesan Truffle Fries. Bag of Donuts is a
dessert not to be missed (they come with dulce de
leche and raspberry sauce dips. You'll be happy, but
groaning afterwards, like me.). Amazing cocktails.

TAVERN
1904 Broadway, Nashville, 615-320-8580
www.mstreetnashville.com/tavern/
CUISINE: Gastro pub; some Asian; some Mexican

DRINKS: Full Bar
SERVING: Lunch and Dinner daily; Brunch on weekends from 10 am; open till 3 am Friday & Saturday
PRICE RANGE: $$ to $$$
NEIGHBORHOOD: Downtown
Wraparound booths create a cozy atmosphere within the lively bar scene in this high-ceilinged room. A half-raised mezzanine level lets you look down on the bar scene while you eat. Later in the evening, they shift to more energetic beat, with DJs cranking out the tunes. (They stay open till about 3 am on Friday and Saturday.) Lots of TVs for the sports-inclined. Has one of the better brunches on weekends. Small plates like wood-grilled artichokes; egg rolls; fried chicken skins; chili scallops. A great selection of creative tacos: fish, lamb, chicken, short ribs. Also an impressive line-up of salads and sandwiches; mahi, tuna salad, lobster sliders, patak bratwurst, as well as a great burger. Main plates include grilled hamburger steak with a fried egg on top; a basket of crispy little fish (cornmeal fried catfish); lots of specialty cocktails. If you're here for brunch, get the White Trash Hash and the Benedict Uno with braised short ribs. The brunches are very busy.

TENNESSEE BREW WORKS
809 Ewing Ave, Nashville, 615-436-0050
www.tnbrew.com
CUISINE: Brewery/Burgers
DRINKS: Beer & Wine Only
SERVING: Lunch/Dinner
PRICE RANGE: $$

NEIGHBORHOOD: Downtown
Basically a brewery serving beers brewed on-site but if you're hungry you can order a burger. Tours available for a small fee. Lots of games to keep the drinkers occupied. Raves for the burgers and beers.

TWO TEN JACK
1900 Eastland Ave #105, Nashville, 615-454-2731
www.twotenjack.com
CUISINE: Ramen
DRINKS: Full Bar
SERVING: Dinner, closed Sun
PRICE RANGE: $$
NEIGHBORHOOD: Lockeland Springs
A Japanese-inspired neighborhood pub that offers a menu of kodawari ramen, skewers & grilled items, sushi and Japanese inspired pub comfort food. Handcrafted cocktails.

URBAN GRUB

2506 12th Ave S, Nashville, 615-679-9342
https://www.urbangrub.net/
CUISINE: Seafood/Southern
DRINKS: Full Bar
SERVING: Dinner, Lunch/Brunch on Sat & Sun,
Closed Mondays
PRICE RANGE: $$$
NEIGHBORHOOD: 12 South District
Modern eatery serving up fresh fish and fine aged
meats. They butcher their own meat, so they're
known for their dry aged beef. Hard to believe, but
this place started as a little car wash and they built it
into a multifaceted space housing a bar, a patio with
woodburning fireplace (and some private fire pits)

and a beer garden. Very friendly atmosphere.
Favorites: Lobster Cakes (the sherry they add to this
dish makes all the difference in the world); Shrimp &
Grits and Ribs. Sides are huge so you can share. Nice
selection of desserts.

VIRAGO
1120 McGavock St, Nashville, 615-254-1902
www.mstreetnashville.com/virago
CUISINE: Japanese; robata grill & sushi bar
DRINKS: Full Bar
SERVING: Dinner nightly from 5
PRICE RANGE: $$$
NEIGHBORHOOD: Downtown; Gulch
Has a strikingly modern design inside with a slanted
ceiling held up by stark metal posts; wood and brick,
recessed lighting. Lobster tacos; crispy Brussels
sprouts; Tsukune chicken meatballs; bacon wrapped
scallops; Mune chicken breast; smoked brisket Udon;
tuffled black grouper; salt & pepper shrimp. There's a
very nice rooftop bar with a view of Downtown, so
go up there if you can.

WHISKEY KITCHEN

118 12th Ave S, Nashville, 615-254-3029
www.mstreetnashville.com
CUISINE: American (New)
DRINKS: Full Bar
SERVING: Lunch, Dinner
PRICE RANGE: $$
NEIGHBORHOOD: Downtown
Popular bar with a menu of tavern grub. Menu
favorites include: Blackbean burger, Braised beef
short ribs and Whiskey brownie cheesecake.

Inside at The Yellow Porch

YELLOW PORCH

734 Thompson Lane, Nashville, 615-386-0260
https://www.theyellowporch.com/
CUISINE: American (New)
DRINKS: Full Bar
SERVING: Lunch & Dinner, Closed Sundays
PRICE RANGE: $$
NEIGHBORHOOD: Berry Hill
A foodies' paradise offering casual dining and an impressive seasonal menu. It's a little dark inside, and for décor they line the walls with black-and-white images of celebrities. Favorites: Pork Chop (one of the best, marinated in sweet tea); Sorghum Infused Duck Breast; Herb Marinated Skillet Chicken. Curated wine list. Desserts should be considered with Drunken Peach Bread Pudding as the top choice.

Outside at The Yellow Porch

NIGHTLIFE

THE 5 SPOT
1006 Forrest Ave., Nashville, 615-650-9333
http://the5spotlive.com/blog/
NEIGHBORHOOD: East Nashville, near Five Points
This long narrow bar with a stage at the far end is a
great spot for dancing, cheap beer, lots of live music,
offering up multiple acts every night except Monday.
There's a modest menu offering a couple of pizzas
and some sandwiches if you want a snack. They have
a gay dance party on the third Friday of every month
called **QDP (Queer Dance Party).**

THE BASEMENT
917 Woodland St, Nashville, 615-645-9174
www.thebasementnashville.com
This small venue books a wide variety of music acts, from country singer to indie bands. Check the web site for schedule. No smoking inside. 21 and over. If you go upstairs, you'll find one of the best indie record stores in town (maybe even the country), **Grimey's New & Preloved Music.**

BASTION
434 Houston St, Nashville, 615-490-8434
www.bastionnashville.com
NEIGHBORHOOD: South Nashville, Wedgewood-Houston
This little warehouse-style bar, connected to the restaurant, is right out of a trailer park, very low-brow but don't let its looks fool you—they serve up highly

creative cocktails, as well as draft beer and wine.
They have nachos if you need a snack. Their Punch of
the Day changes every day, so give it a try.

BEARDED IRIS BREWING TAPROOM
101 Van Buren St, Nashville, 615-928-7988
www.beardedirisbrewing.com
NEIGHBORHOOD: East Germantown
Brewery taproom serving rotating selection of old-
world style beer. Comfortable atmosphere with velvet
couches, large chandelier and an old pool table.
Known for their IPA (India Pale Ale). Usually there's
a food truck parked outside that serves up very tasty
food if you're hungry.

BLUEBIRD CAFÉ
4104 Hillsboro Pike, Nashville, 615-383-1461
www.bluebirdcafe.com
If you're a singer or a songwriter, performing here is
like a "coming of age" experience. They usually have
2 shows a night. The cozy (OK, tight and crowded)
room that seats only 100 lucky customers is actually a
good thing, not a bad thing. You feel like you're
seeing tomorrow's stars, and in many cases, you
really are. If you're a fan of the show "Nashville,"
you've seen what you think is this place on TV.
Though they perform on a set (accurate even down to
the line of lights strung along the bar), it's uncanny
how well they captured this place. The walls are
plastered with pictures of some of the thousands of
musicians who've performed here. You'll want to
reserve a seat, but reservations open usually Monday
at 8 a.m. for the shows that week. They go fast. They

serve food, but it's not that good, so eat elsewhere and come here for the show. Plan on showing up early. They will give your reserved seat to someone else if you're a minute late.

BOBBY'S IDLE HOUR
9 Music Square S, Nashville, 615-649-8530
www.bobbysidlehour.com
A dive bar with live music. Wednesday and Thursday night jams. A favorite hangout of local songwriters. People on the way up in the music business gather here, as well as people on the way down.

BONGO JAVA
2007 Belmont Blvd, Nashville, 615-385-5282
www.bongojava.com
NEIGHBORHOOD: Belmont, Hillsboro
Right across the street from Belmont University is this place that's a hangout for lots of artists, students, musicians and those who want to be around them. You can mix and mingle with them over a cup of coffee or a snack. Try the Juanita Burrita (3 eggs,

grilled onions & jalapenos with chipotle cream cheese & jack cheese in a tortilla—comes with hashbrowns and house salsa). They also have burgers, several sandwiches, tacos, grilled cheese, salads. Above the coffeeshop is the **Bongo After Hours Theatre**, which showcases theatre, musical events, improve, classes and workshops.

BUTCHERTOWN HALL
1416 4th Ave N, Nashville, 615-454-3634
www.butchertownhall.com
NEIGHBORHOOD: Germantown
Rustic-chic hall that serves incredible cocktails and brews. Some come to drink, others to eat – nice selection of Mexican-inspired eats like tacos and queso. But the beer is the star attraction here, though there are some nicely prices good wines as well.

CHAUHAN ALE & MASALA HOUSE
123 12th Ave N, Nashville, 615-242-8426
www.chauhannashville.com
NEIGHBORHOOD: Downtown
Located in a refurbished brick garage, this place offers a menu of creative Indian fare and exceptional cocktails. Bar offers a worldwide selection of wine and spirits and crafted cocktails.

CRYING WOLF
823 Woodland St, Nashville, 615-953-6715
www.thecryingwolf.com
A no-frills bar that also serves burgers.

EAST NASHVILLE

Across the Cumberland River is the hippest area of town called East Nashville. This is where the more cutting edge segment of the population lives and works and hangs out (the artists, the musicians, etc.), and you'd be doing yourself a disservice if you don't venture over here. It's East Nashville that's giving the town its international press, not Downtown. Just as in any other town where these people congregate, the restaurants, coffeehouses, cafes, nightclubs, lounges and shops have sprouted up to serve their needs.

THE END

2219 Elliston Pl, Nashville, 615-321-4457
www.endnashville.com
This is another great venue where you can hear excellent indie rock bands, both local and national.

GRAND OLE OPRY HOUSE

2804 Opryland Drive, Nashville, 615-871-6779
www.opry.com

The live-performance radio program that put Nashville on the map is still going strong, even after the horrendous 2010 flood that wrecked the building. All is well, however, in the refurbished venue. Even if you HATE country music, you've got to make an effort to squeeze this into your itinerary. There's a backstage tour of the facility. You'll be able to stand onstage where thousands of legendary performers have stood "in the circle." You'll learn the history of the Opry (it started at the Ryman Auditorium downtown) and how it developed, and all of it is very interesting. You'll get to see the old studio where "Hee Haw" was filmed, and you'll get to see a show running a couple of hours featuring a steady stream of entertainers, comedians, singers. This will likely be the standout experience of your visit if you make the plunge and do it. It's something you'll never forget as long as you live.

THE HIGH WATT
1 Cannery Row, Nashville, 615-251-3020
www.mercylounge.com
A cozy little club housed in a century-old former cannery showcases local up and coming bands and national talents. 500 capacity music venue with a back bar that features pool tables and booth seating.

HONKEY TONK CENTRAL

329 Broadway, Nashville, 615-742-9095
www.honkytonkcentral.com
Very busy 3-story pub featuring live music. Huge bar and pub menu. Large TV for sports fans. It's a big-time tourist trap.

HURRY BACK

2212 Elliston Pl, Nashville, 615-915-0764
www.hurry-back.com
Great selection of rare and craft beers. Bar fare menu. TVs and big projector for sports. Outdoor seating.

MELROSE BILLIARDS

2600 8th Ave S, Nashville, 615-678-5489
www.dirtymelrose.com
This is a true dive bar filled with lots of old-time regulars. Cheap prices, pool tables, ping pong, and

snooker. Everybody from construction workers to studio musicians.

NO. 308
407 Gallatin Ave, Nashville, 615-650-7344
www.bar308.com/
Trendy late-night hangout serving craft cocktails. Patio seating and popular happy hour. (Get the 308 sliders if you're hungry.)

OAK BAR
THE HERMITAGE HOTEL
231 Sixth Ave N, Nashville, 615-345-7116
http://www.capitolgrillenashville.com/oak-bar.asp
NEIGHBORHOOD: Downtown; Lower Broadway
Though I'm putting this in the nightlife chapter, it's also a perfect place to meet for a drink before dinner, or to come when winding down the evening for a Cognac after dinner or a show. Opens at 11:30 for drinks and also has a casual menu (fried pickles; smoked bologna sandwich; Granny's deviled eggs; hunter's plate of house-cured smoked meats and pickled items; Brunswick stew; BBQ shrimp; the Tennessee Stack is two 4-ounce Double H beef patties with cheddar, pepper jelly, sweet onion and hot mustard), and is open for happy hour from 4:30 to 6:30.

PINEWOOD SOCIAL
33 Peabody St, Nashville, 615-751-8111
www.pinewoodsocial.com
Trendy industrial-chic hangout open all day. The location used to be a trolley car depot, so it has a

funky charm. The place is divided into three parts—couches in the front section are nice for a cup of Crema coffee in the morning; the middle section is great for innovative cocktails and some food (the catfish sandwich is my favorite); the section in the back is where they have vintage bowling lanes and karaoke. In the summer, there's even a pool on the patio.

THE PATTERSON HOUSE
1711 Division St, Nashville, 615-636-7724
www.thepattersonnashville.com
This dark, luxurious bar throwing off a speakeasy vibe and sporting vintage chandeliers and rows of bookshelves serves delicious old-fashioned cocktails

late into the night. There's a velvet curtain you pass through, a bar in the center with stools and a series of booths against the walls lit by candles. They are very serious about the craft cocktails served here, down to the point that they make their own bitters in house. Bacon Old Fashioned has maple syrup in it; the classic Sidecar is served, one of my favorite drinks. The small plate menu items are all made to order, from the potato chips to the truffled deviled eggs; beef sliders & tater tots; cinnamon sugar donuts; fig & prosciutto flatbread (and don't overlook the donut holes). One of my all-time favorite places in Nashville.

ROBERT'S WESTERN WORLD
416B Broadway, Nashville, 615-244-9552
www.robertswesternworld.com

NEIGHBORHOOD: Downtown
In Nashville, when you say you're going "honky-tonking," it means you're going out on the town. This is one of the best places to do that. A super variety of great musical acts fills their schedule. You can't miss their big sign right on Broadway with the lit up guitar. Also has good white trash food: fried Bolonga sandwiches, grilled cheese, cheap burgers that are so juicy and flavorful, really good hot dogs. I don't know anybody who doesn't absolutely love this place. When it's really crowded on Friday and Saturday nights, go to the back-alley entrance next to the Ryman Auditorium where you'll find a doorman who's checking IDs, but you can still get in with less hassle.

SANTA'S PUB
2225 Bransford Ave, Nashville, 615-593-1872
www.santaspub.com
Busy dive bar located in a triple-wide trailer. Holiday décor all year with cheap beer and karaoke that seems to be continuous. You can miss the mural of the Santa on the motorcycle on the front of the building. Cash only.

SPRINGWATER
115 27th Ave N, Nashville, 615-320-0345
www.springwatersupperclub.com
My younger readers won't know who he is, but Jimmy Hoffa used to hang out here in one of the best beer-only dive bars in Nashville that once-upon-a-time was a speakeasy. It's located next to Centennial Park. You'll encounter a bunch of drunks spending

their Social Security checks, college kids looking to slum it. But the jukebox is good and they have arcade games.

THE STAGE ON BROADWAY
412 Broadway, Nashville, 615-726-0504
www.thestageonbroadway.com
A Honky-Tonk that mixes the flavor of Texas with Nashville. Live country music and a dance floor. Never a cover charge. Country music for people wearing flip flops.

STATION INN
402 12th Ave S, Nashville, 615-255-3307
www.stationinn.com
NEIGHBORHOOD: Downtown; Gulch
When you first get a glimpse of this plain concrete building, you get the sense that this place doesn't really belong here because the Gulch area has become

so trendy, with expensive new condos rising around it. But this is one of the top destinations in town because of its excellent bluegrass and old-time shows that continue to attract crowds, as they have for many years. Every time I go there, I hear brilliant music, especially bluegrass and Western swing. On any given night, while you down your Bud Light and eat popcorn, you might see Ronnie Bowman, Guy Clark or another, younger player everyone's going to be talking about in a couple years.

THE SUTLER SALOON
2600 8th Ave S #109, Nashville, 615-840-6124
www.thesutler.com
Rustic-chic late-night hangout serving craft cocktails and Southern fare. Live music.

TOOTSIE'S ORCHID LOUNGE
422 Broadway, Nashville, 615-726-0463
www.tootsies.net/

One of Nashville's original Honky Tonks. The place is filled with memories and photos of bands that have played there. Great place to hang out and watch the locals mingle with the musicians who fill the place. Willie Nelson grew up signing here and Patsy Cline used to drink here. Kristofferson used to hang out here as well.

WHISKEY KITCHEN
118 12th Ave S, Nashville, 615-254-3029
www.mstreetnashville.com
Busy and welcoming watering hole featuring a menu of global whiskeys and tavern fare. This is a good place to begin your tour of the area's nightlife opportunities.

INDEX

www.ingramcontent.com/pod-product-compliance
Ingram Content Group UK Ltd.
Pitfield, Milton Keynes, MK11 3LW, UK
UKHW021647190726
13853UKWH00001B/103